100 Bible Heroes
100 Bible Songs

Created by Stephen Elkins

Illustrated by Aleksey and Olga Ivanov

THOMAS NELSON
Since 1798

NASHVILLE   DALLAS   MEXICO CITY   RIO DE JANEIRO   BEIJING

Table of Contents

Heroes in red • Songs in black

Aaron

Two are better than one. . . . If one falls down, his friend can help him up. ECCLESIASTES 4:9–10

from EXODUS 3–4

AARON WAS A GOOD HELPER.

Aaron had a very special younger brother. His name was Moses. When God gave Moses a big job to do, Aaron helped him do his work. God told Moses to go to Egypt and tell Pharaoh to free the Israelites.

Since Moses said he wasn't good at speaking in front of others, Aaron went along to help. He had a wonderful speaking voice. Together, Aaron and Moses told Pharaoh the message from God: "Let my people go!"

I WILL BE A GOOD HELPER.

My Family Matters

Two are better than one, child.
If one falls down, yes, two are better than one, child,
'Cause his friend can help him up.

Heroes are good helpers. That's certainly true when we help a brother or sister. God loves a good helper!

Abel

from GENESIS 4

ABEL DID WHAT PLEASED THE LORD.

Two sons of Adam and Eve were very different from one another. Cain was the oldest son. He was a farmer, and Abel was a shepherd. But that wasn't the only difference. Abel pleased God by doing what was right. Cain did not!

When it was time to give God an offering, Cain did not give his best to God. But Abel did! Abel knew that God should get only our best. He gave God the best from his flock. God was pleased with Abel!

I WILL DO WHAT PLEASES THE LORD.

8

What Pleases the Lord

Live as children of the light.
Find out what pleases the Lord.

MY SCRIPTURE SONG • MY SCRIPTURE SONG
CD 1
SONG 2

Heroes find out what pleases God, and they do it! God is pleased when we obey His word.

Abigail

Make every effort to live in peace with all men and to be holy; without holiness no one will see the LORD. HEBREWS 12:14

from
1 SAMUEL 25

ABIGAIL WAS A PEACEMAKER.

Abigail had a foolish husband named Nabal. He had insulted David, a leader of Israel. This made David so angry that he planned to kill Nabal. When Abigail heard about David's plan, she took food to him to make peace for Nabal.

Even though Nabal was wrong, Abigail helped David to see that it would be wrong for him to kill Nabal. David's heart was changed. Abigail had brought peace to an angry leader!

I WILL BE A PEACEMAKER.

Live in Peace

Make every effort to live in peace
With all men and to be holy.

Heroes are peacemakers who help others to get along. God has promised to bless the peacemakers!

Abraham

The LORD is faithful to all his promises and loving toward all he has made. PSALM 145:13

from
GENESIS 12; 15; 22

ABRAHAM BELIEVED GOD.

God made three very important promises to Abraham. One, God promised Abraham his own country. Two, God promised Abraham a son, even though he was very old. And three, God promised Abraham that the Messiah would come from his family.

Even though these were big promises, Abraham believed God would do what He said! That is why he is called "the father of all who believe." And yes, God kept His promises. Abraham's country was called Canaan, his son was called Isaac, and the Messiah was called Jesus!

I WILL BELIEVE GOD.

The Lord Is Faithful

The Lord is faithful to all His promises
And loving toward all He has made.

Heroes believe God. It's not enough to believe in God. We must believe that the promises of God found in the Bible are true.

Adam

ADAM WORKED FOR THE LORD.

After God made the earth and all creatures, big and small, He created Adam. He placed him in a perfect garden home. But Adam needed something to do, even if it was a perfect place. So God gave him a job!

The world was filled with animals that had no names. It became Adam's job to name them. So one by one, the animals came. "I'll call you hippopotamus," Adam may have said. "And I'll call you monkey." Adam named them all, a job well done! After all, he was working for the Lord!

I WILL WORK FOR THE LORD.

Working for the Lord

Whatever, whatever you do,
Work at it with all your heart,
As working for the Lord and not for men.

Heroes work as if working for the Lord. Some jobs are big. Some are small. But every job should be done as if we are working for the Lord!

Amos

As for God, his way is perfect; the word of the LORD is flawless. 2 SAMUEL 22:31

from the book of AMOS

AMOS SPOKE UP FOR WHAT IS RIGHT.

Most people may have thought Amos was unimportant. Amos was a keeper of sheep. But in God's eyes, he was a mighty prophet. God had something important for Amos to say to the people of Israel. When Amos spoke for God, the message was full of power!

"You are doing bad things," Amos told the people. "You have forgotten how to worship God, and He is not pleased. So change your ways and obey Him!" But the people ignored God's messenger. And soon Israel was taken captive.

I WILL SPEAK UP FOR WHAT IS RIGHT.

His Way Is Perfect

Lots of ways to go, lots of ways you know.
As for God, His way is perfect.

Heroes speak up for what is right. It is right for everyone to worship God and follow Him.

Andrew

"Come, follow me," Jesus said, *"and I will make you fishers of men."* MARK 1:17

from JOHN 1:35–41

ANDREW LED OTHERS TO JESUS.

One day Andrew heard Jesus say, "Come, and I will make you fishers of men!" Right away, he left his net and rushed to follow Jesus. He knew in his heart that Jesus was the Savior. So what did he do next?

He told his brother, Peter. Peter believed too! Together, they followed Jesus. Andrew told many people about Jesus. He wanted everyone to know about God's special love for them!

I WILL LEAD OTHERS TO JESUS.

Come, Follow Me

Come, follow Me,
And I will make you fishers of men.

Heroes lead others to Jesus. They tell about His love and grace.

Anna

For God so loved the world that he gave his one and only Son. JOHN 3:16

from LUKE 2:36–40

ANNA TOLD EVERYONE THAT JESUS WAS THE SAVIOR.

Anna was a prophetess. She spent her days in the temple fasting and praying. She never left the temple. Widowed for many years, Anna was now 84 years old.

After Jesus was born, Mary and Joseph took Him to the temple. Anna was there as she always was. She saw the child and knew He was the Messiah. She gave thanks to God. And to all who were looking for the coming Messiah, she spoke about Jesus.

I WILL TELL EVERYONE THAT JESUS IS THE SAVIOR.

God So Loved the World

For God so loved the world
That He gave His one and only Son.

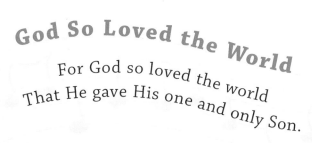

Heroes speak to everyone about Jesus. They tell of His love and saving grace.

21

Apollos

How good and pleasant it is when brothers live together in unity! PSALM 133:1

from ACTS 18;
1 CORINTHIANS 3

APOLLOS WORKED WITH OTHERS TO WIN THE LOST TO JESUS.

Paul traveled many places spreading the gospel message. As he traveled, another man of God was working to do the same. His name was Apollos. He preached the gospel with great power in Corinth. He, too, encouraged many to believe in Christ.

Paul explained that he may plant a seed by teaching the lost, and Apollos may water it, but God is the One who makes it grow. Paul and Apollos knew that working together was the best way to win the lost. Paul taught, "We are all servants of Christ. Each of us has a role to play. Let us all work together for the Lord."

I WILL WORK WITH OTHERS TO WIN THE LOST TO JESUS.

Brothers in Unity

How good and pleasant it is
When brothers live together in unity!
Makes a better world, it's true.

Heroes work together to build God's kingdom. When we work together, others come to know and believe in Jesus.

Asa

The prayer of a righteous man is powerful and effective. JAMES 5:16

from
1 KINGS 15;
2 CHRONICLES
14–16

ASA PRAYED FOR GOD'S HELP.

Asa was a very strong king. He told his people to obey the Lord. He trusted God to give him guidance and victory.

When it came time for his country to go into battle, Asa did what strong kings do: he prayed. "Lord, it is nothing for You to help us this day." Asa knew that any problem in God's hand was a small problem. And God answered. The victory was won!

I WILL PRAY FOR GOD'S HELP.

The Prayer of a Righteous Man

The prayer of a righteous man
Is powerful and effective.

Heroes know they must depend on God for their strength. Asking God for wisdom and courage to do right—this is a hero's prayer.

25

Balaam

from NUMBERS 22–24

BALAAM CHOSE TO SPEAK BLESSINGS, NOT CURSES.

As Israel prepared for battle, the enemy king sent messengers to ask Balaam to curse God's people. Balaam refused. But after a while, Balaam agreed to go hear what the king had to say.

When they came to a narrow place, Balaam's donkey would not go any farther. Balaam beat the donkey. God caused the donkey to say, "Why do you beat me?" Then Balaam saw the angel God sent to block his way. The angel told Balaam, "Go, but say only what I tell you to say." Even though the king offered great rewards for Balaam to curse God's people, Balaam only said good things about them.

I WILL SPEAK BLESSINGS, NOT CURSES.

26

Choose Life!

I have set before you life and death.
I have set before you blessings and curses.
Now choose life, now choose life.

Heroes choose to say nice things about God's people! Even when others are being unkind, heroes say the things God would want them to say.

27

Barnabas

You hear, O LORD, the desire of the afflicted; you encourage them, and you listen to their cry. PSALM 10:17

from ACTS 4:36; 11–15

BARNABAS ENCOURAGED OTHERS.

Though his name was Joseph, he was called Barnabas, which means "son of encouragement." Barnabas loved God and encouraged others to love God too.

Barnabas traveled with Paul to encourage new believers. They spent a whole year teaching the people of Antioch and helping the new church grow. Barnabas encouraged everyone!

I WILL ENCOURAGE OTHERS.

You Encourage Them, I Know

You, O Lord, hear the call of the hurting.
You encourage them, I know.

Heroes encourage others. By helping, by sharing, by listening, they encourage others by showing God's love.

29

Bartimaeus

Whatever you ask for in prayer, believe that you have received it, and it will be yours. MARK 11:24

from LUKE 18:35–43

BARTIMAEUS BELIEVED THE LORD COULD DO ANYTHING.

Bartimaeus was blind. As he sat by the roadside begging, he heard that Jesus was passing by. He cried out above the crowd, "Jesus! Have mercy!" He shouted louder. Then the people took him to Jesus. Jesus asked, "What do you want Me to do for you?"

Bartimaeus believed that all things were possible with Jesus, even the healing of his blind eyes. With great faith Bartimaeus said, "Lord, heal me!" What joy filled his heart when Jesus said, "Receive your sight. Your faith has healed you!"

I WILL BELIEVE THE LORD CAN DO ANYTHING.

Believe It, Receive It

Whatever you ask for in prayer,
Believe it now.

*Heroes believe that God can do all things. So they ask God,
believing He is able to answer their prayers.*

31

Barzillai

The LORD is my helper;
I will not be afraid. HEBREWS 13:6

from
2 SAMUEL
17:27–29; 19:32–39

BARZILLAI HELPED
THOSE IN NEED.

King David and his people had traveled in a desert. They needed food and rest. An older man named Barzillai helped them. He and his friends brought food and other things to help David and his people. God was pleased!

David's people were now refreshed, and they won the next battle. Barzillai's help had made a difference. To thank him, David said, "Come to Jerusalem, and I will take care of you!" But Barzillai wanted to stay in his hometown. David blessed his loyal friend Barzillai for his kindness.

I WILL HELP
THOSE IN NEED.

The Lord Is My Helper

The Lord is my helper.
The Lord is my helper;
I will not be afraid.

Heroes help those in need. They look for opportunities to serve others. They share what they have to help others in a difficult time.

Benjamin

Blessed are the people whose God is the L<small>ORD</small>. P<small>SALM</small> 144:15

from
GENESIS 35;
37; 42–43

BENJAMIN WAS A BLESSING TO HIS FAMILY.

Benjamin was the youngest of Jacob's 12 sons. His brother Joseph had been betrayed by his other brothers and sold as a slave. Their father thought Joseph was dead. His heart was broken, so he loved young Benjamin even more. Benjamin's name means "son of my right hand." Benjamin was a blessing to his father.

Years later, Benjamin was reunited with Joseph. When Joseph saw Benjamin, he cried tears of joy. Benjamin was a blessing to his brother too.

I WILL BE A BLESSING TO MY FAMILY.

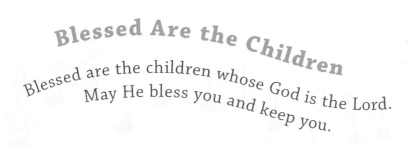

Blessed Are the Children

Blessed are the children whose God is the Lord.
May He bless you and keep you.

MY SCRIPTURE SONG • MY SCRIPTURE SONG
CD 1
SONG 15

Heroes are blessings to their families. They are kind and respectful.
They know this is the way God wants them to be.

Bezalel

from
EXODUS 26; 31

BEZALEL USED HIS ABILITIES
TO HONOR GOD.

Miracles happen! The Israelites had walked between walls of water through the Red Sea. God had just written the Ten Commandments in stone when He said to Moses, "Now build a meeting tent. Make a fine table and lampstand to go inside. I have given Bezalel the ability to help you."

God had given Bezalel the skill to make beautiful things. Just as God had told Moses, Bezalel oversaw the building of the tabernacle tent and crafted many vessels of worship. God had supplied the ability!

I WILL USE MY ABILITIES
TO HONOR GOD.

May the God of Peace

May the God of peace equip you
With everything good for doing His will.

Heroes use their God-given abilities to honor Him. They give back to God a measure of what He has given them.

The Boy with Loaves and Fishes

Share with others, for with such sacrifices God is pleased. HEBREWS 13:16

from
JOHN 6:5–13

THE BOY SHARED WITH OTHERS.

Five thousand people followed Jesus to a hillside. It was late in the day, so they were very hungry. Seeing their need, Jesus said to His disciples, "Feed them."

"We can't feed this crowd!" they said. But close by was a boy who was willing to share. He gave his lunch to Jesus and His disciples. Five thousand people were fed that day with five small loaves of bread and two small fish. A miracle happened that day because a boy shared his food!

I WILL SHARE WITH OTHERS.

Sharing Is Caring

Sharing is really caring, caring about the friends
you know. And sharing is truly daring,
To show the Lord you love Him so!

Heroes share what they have with others. They know that everything they have belongs to God. So they share His blessings with others.

Caleb

from
NUMBERS 13–14;
JOSHUA 14:6–15

CALEB TRUSTED IN THE LORD.

Moses called Caleb and 11 other men to scout the land of Canaan. They would give a report to the people of Israel. Ten of the men returned and spread fear among the people. But Caleb said, "Do not be afraid. God is with us. Let's take the land!"

But the people would not trust God. Fear caused them to wander in the desert for 40 years! Because of Caleb's trust, God promised a portion of the land to Caleb and his descendants. When the Israelites finally took the land, Joshua blessed Caleb by giving him the whole city of Hebron.

I WILL TRUST IN THE LORD.

Trust in the Lord with All Your Heart

Trust in the Lord with all your heart.
Trust in the Lord with all your heart and soul.

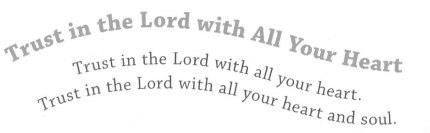

Heroes trust in the Lord. They trust Him even when others are afraid. They persuade others to trust God too!

The Centurion

THE CENTURION HAD AMAZING FAITH.

There was once a Roman captain, called a centurion, who asked Jesus to heal his servant. Jesus said, "I'll go and heal him." But the centurion said, "Lord, I'm not good enough to have You in my house. If You just command him to be healed, he will be healed."

Jesus was amazed at the centurion's faith. He said, "Go! It will be done just as you believed it would." And the Bible tells us the centurion's servant was healed at that very hour.

I WILL HAVE AMAZING FAITH!

Mustard Seed Faith

If you have faith as small as a mustard seed,
You can say to this mountain,
"Move from here to there."

Heroes believe that Jesus has authority over sickness. They ask Him to heal those who are ill.

Cornelius

My brothers, as believers in our glorious LORD Jesus Christ, don't show favoritism. JAMES 2:1

from ACTS 10

CORNELIUS BELIEVED THAT GOD DID NOT SHOW FAVORITISM.

Cornelius was a tough Roman captain. He prayed to God every day, but he didn't know about Jesus. One day an angel appeared and told Cornelius to send for Peter. At that time, it was against Jewish practice for Peter to visit Cornelius, a Gentile, in his home. Cornelius sent for him anyway.

God told Peter to go tell Cornelius about Jesus. Because Peter obeyed, Cornelius and his friends and family learned about Jesus. Peter learned a big lesson too: God does not show favoritism. He accepts people from every nation.

I WILL NOT SHOW FAVORITISM.

God Sees the Heart

My brothers, my brothers,
As believers in Jesus Christ,
Don't show favoritism! No! No! No!

Heroes do not show favoritism. They respect all people as children of God, created in His image.

Damaris

Everyone who calls on the name of the Lord will be saved. ROMANS 10:13

from
ACTS 17:22–34

DAMARIS REFUSED FALSE GODS
TO FOLLOW JESUS.

The Greeks had many gods. They worshiped Zeus as the chief of all their gods. They worshiped goddesses like Artemis or Isis. They even worshiped a god of time named Chronos. So when Paul preached in Athens, some thought that his God was just another god.

Damaris was there when Paul preached. When she heard the gospel of Jesus, she believed! Some laughed and made fun. But she chose to follow Jesus Christ!

I WILL REFUSE FALSE GODS
TO FOLLOW JESUS.

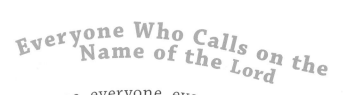

Everyone Who Calls on the Name of the Lord

Everyone, everyone, everyone who calls on the Name of the Lord—they will be saved forever!

 Heroes follow Jesus. Even when others may laugh or ridicule them, they stand firm in their faith.

Daniel

Three times a day he got down on his knees and prayed, giving thanks to his God. DANIEL 6:10

from
DANIEL 6

DANIEL PRAYED,
NO MATTER WHAT.

Daniel was a young leader who loved God. But the men he commanded did not love God. They were jealous of Daniel. Knowing that Daniel prayed three times a day, they made an evil plan to get him in trouble.

They tricked the king into passing a bad law. The law said that no one was to pray to God for 30 days. But Daniel still prayed, no matter what! When they found him praying, Daniel was thrown into a lions' den. How frightening! But Daniel prayed there too! And the Lord kept him safe.

I WILL PRAY, NO MATTER WHAT.

Three Times a Day

Three times a day
He got down on his knees.
(Yeah, yeah!)

MY SCRIPTURE SONG · MY SCRIPTURE SONG · CD 1 SONG 22

Heroes pray, no matter what. If the day is good and full of blessings, they thank the Lord. If it's bad or frightening, they pray for protection.

David

from 1 SAMUEL 17

DAVID CALLED ON THE NAME OF THE LORD.

"Send someone out to fight me!" Goliath shouted. Israel's army sat fearful and still. No one would dare face him. He was way too big! But after 40 days of his dares, someone stepped out.

It was David, the shepherd boy. He chose five smooth stones and walked up to the giant. "You come against me with a sword," David said, "but I come against you in the name of the Lord!" David hurled a stone with his sling. It hit the mark. Down went Goliath!

I WILL CALL ON THE NAME OF THE LORD.

The Name of the Lord

The name of the Lord is a strong tower;
The righteous run to it and are safe.

Heroes know that God is bigger than any problem. Whether it's a giant problem, like Goliath, or just a little problem, call on the Lord to help you.

Deborah

I will sing to the Lord, I will sing; I will make music to the Lord, the God of Israel. Judges 5:3

from JUDGES 4–5

DEBORAH LISTENED TO GOD.

Deborah loved the Lord and did what pleased Him. She was a judge in Israel. Many people sought her advice. Her words were fair and just.

When a mighty army threatened Israel, God spoke to Deborah. She listened! He advised Israel's army to fight. God would be with them! Deborah helped lead Israel to victory. She gave thanks to God and sang, "I will sing to the Lord." Because Deborah listened to God, Israel had peace for 40 years!

I WILL LISTEN TO GOD.

Holy, Holy Is His Name

MY SCRIPTURE SONG · MY SCRIPTURE SONG · CD 1 SONG 24

Holy Lord, whatever the day may bring,
Whatever the song we sing,
We sing to You.

Heroes listen to God. He speaks through the Bible. He speaks through the events in our lives. So when God speaks, listen!

Dorcas

Give, and it will be given to you.

LUKE 6:38

from ACTS 9:36–42

DORCAS GAVE TO THOSE IN NEED.

Dorcas was a follower of Jesus. She was known in Joppa for her kindness and generosity. One day Dorcas became ill and died.

Her friends sent for Peter. When he arrived, the widows stood around him, crying and showing him the clothes Dorcas had made.

Peter knelt near Dorcas and prayed. Then he said to her, "Dorcas, get up!" And she sat up! She was alive! Dorcas had given her life to serving others. Now God had given new life to her.

I WILL GIVE TO THOSE IN NEED.

Give!

Give, and it will be given to you, given to you.
Give, and it will be given to you, my friend.

Heroes give. And by giving, they receive this promise: "Give, and it will be given to you."

Elijah

How awesome is the LORD Most High.

PSALM 47:2

from
1 KINGS 18:20–46

ELIJAH SERVED
THE ONE TRUE GOD.

Elijah was the only servant of the one true God on Mount Carmel that day. He was a bit outnumbered. There were 450 servants of Baal, a false god. Elijah said to the people, "Let us prove whose is the true God."

So they built two altars. They placed a sacrifice on each one. Elijah said, "The god who sends fire from heaven is the one true God." The prophets of Baal prayed to their god, but no fire came. Then Elijah prayed to his God. A huge blast of fire fell from heaven and burned up the sacrifice, the wood, and even the stones in the altar! How awesome was Elijah's one true God!

I WILL SERVE THE
ONE TRUE GOD.

How Awesome Is the Lord

How awesome, how awesome is our God!
He is an awesome God!

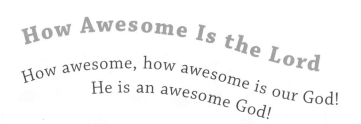 *Heroes serve the one true God, even when they are the only ones in the crowd who believe.*

Elisha

from
1 KINGS 19:16–19;
2 KINGS 2:1–15

ELISHA LEARNED
FROM OTHER BELIEVERS.

Elisha was Elijah's good helper. They worked side by side serving the Lord. Elijah instructed Elisha as his faith was growing.

When Elijah knew his time on earth was nearing the end, he said to Elisha, "Tell me what I can do for you." Elisha said, "Let there be a double blessing of your spirit on me!" Elijah answered, "If you see me being taken from you, you will have it." Suddenly a chariot of fire pulled by fiery horses appeared and took Elijah to heaven. Elisha received the double blessing of Elijah's wise spirit!

I WILL LEARN FROM
OTHER BELIEVERS.

God Will Instruct Us

God will instruct us;
He will teach us
In the way we should go.

*Heroes accept godly instruction. They learn from those who trust
the Lord and live according to the Bible!*

Elizabeth

I trust in you, O LORD; I say, "You are my God." My times are in your hands. PSALM 31:14–15

from
LUKE 1:5–56

ELIZABETH BELIEVED GOD'S TIMING IS PERFECT.

Elizabeth was a young Jewish woman who married a man named Zechariah. Zechariah was a priest, and together they served the Lord faithfully. Elizabeth and Zechariah asked the Lord for a child. But days turned into years, and no child came.

Then God touched Elizabeth's life with a miracle. Though she was old, Elizabeth discovered that she was going to be a mother! Her son would prepare the way for Jesus' coming. Her son became known as John the Baptist. God's timing was perfect!

I WILL BELIEVE GOD'S TIMING IS PERFECT.

My Times Are in Your Hands

But I trust in You, O Lord; I say, "You are my God."
My times are in Your hands;
They're in Your hands, Lord.

Heroes believe that God's timing is always perfect. The events of our lives happen so that His will may be done!

Enoch

I will live with them and walk among them, and I will be their God, and they will be my people. 2 CORINTHIANS 6:16

from
GENESIS 5:18–23

ENOCH WALKED WITH THE LORD.

The Bible says that Enoch walked with the Lord for 300 years! Does that mean he walked around nonstop for 300 years? No, "walking with the Lord" means pleasing the Lord. We can please the Lord by having a strong faith, doing what's right, and giving our time and efforts to Him.

Enoch walked with the Lord, and we can too.

I WILL WALK WITH THE LORD.

Come Walk with Me, Lord

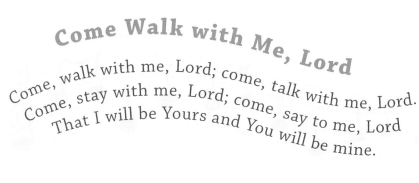

Come, walk with me, Lord; come, talk with me, Lord.
Come, stay with me, Lord; come, say to me, Lord
That I will be Yours and You will be mine.

Heroes walk with the Lord. They please the Lord by being faithful, giving to God, and doing what is right.

Esther

And who knows but that you have come to royal position for such a time as this? ESTHER 4:14

from the book of ESTHER

ESTHER SHOWED COURAGE BY DOING WHAT WAS RIGHT.

The Jews had a terrible enemy. His name was Haman. He had a terrible plan to kill all the Jews. Only Queen Esther could stop him. But to do so, she would have to go before the king, without being invited. This was against the law.

She asked the Jews to fast for three days. "Then," she said, "I will go in to see the king, even if he kills me." When Esther went in, the king was pleased! Finally, she told the king about Haman's evil plan, and the Jews were saved!

I WILL SHOW COURAGE BY DOING WHAT IS RIGHT.

For Such a Time as This

For such a time as this,
God brought us here to sing.

Heroes show courage. They do what is right and leave the outcome to the Lord.

Ethan

For the LORD is good . . . his faithfulness continues through all generations. PSALM 100:5

from
PSALM 89

ETHAN BELIEVED GOD WAS FAITHFUL TO HIS PROMISES.

God had made a promise. But Ethan was confused. Why was God taking so long to fulfill His promise? He knew God had promised that someone from David's family would always be king. But where was this person?

So Ethan prayed, "I will make known Your faithfulness to all generations." Ethan had faith that God would honor His Word. So he waited. And one day an heir of David *did* come to reign forever. His name is Jesus!

I WILL BELIEVE GOD IS FAITHFUL TO HIS PROMISES.

Shout for Joy!

Shout for joy to the Lord, all the earth.
Worship the Lord with gladness;
Come before Him with joyful songs.

Heroes know the Lord is faithful. When God makes a promise, He always keeps it. That's why heroes tell others about God's faithfulness!

67

Eve

from GENESIS 2–3

EVE WAS CREATED TO FULFILL GOD'S PURPOSE.

God saw Adam sitting alone in the Garden of Eden and said, "It is not good for the man to be alone." So God caused Adam to fall asleep. Then God removed a rib from Adam's side. From that rib God made Eve, the first woman.

Not only was Eve the first woman, she was also the first wife and the first mother. And when Satan deceived her, she was the first sinner. But being the first sinner, she was the first to receive God's grace. God promised that through her children a Savior would come who would defeat Satan. Eve fulfilled God's purpose.

I WAS CREATED TO FULFILL GOD'S PURPOSE.

God Created

In the beginning! Oh, in the beginning!
In the beginning
God created the heavens and the earth.

Heroes know they were created for a purpose. They were created to serve God.

Ezekiel

There will be showers of blessing.

Ezekiel 34:26

from
EZEKIEL 33–34

EZEKIEL KNEW THAT ALL BLESSINGS COME FROM THE LORD.

He also knew that bad choices can bring big trouble. So he reminded God's people to make good choices. He asked them to seek God, because without Him there would be no blessing. But they ignored Ezekiel's warning.

This made God very unhappy. Their bad choices led to their capture by the Babylonians. But Ezekiel still proclaimed God's message. "God will judge the people. He will send down showers of blessing for those who follow Him," he said. Ezekiel brought hope to God's people.

I KNOW THAT ALL BLESSINGS COME FROM THE LORD.

Showers of Blessing

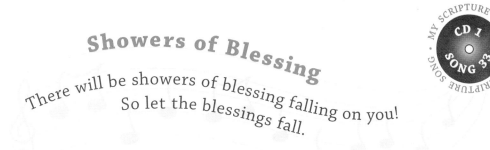

There will be showers of blessing falling on you!
So let the blessings fall.

Heroes know that good choices can bring blessings. And all blessings come down from our Father in heaven.

Ezra

from
EZRA 7

EZRA LOVED AND OBEYED GOD'S WORD.

Ezra spent his life studying God's Word and teaching it to others. Because of this, the Bible says "the hand of the Lord his God was on him."

The Jews had been captives of the Babylonians for many years. Then Babylon was defeated by the Persians. The Persians agreed to let the Jews go back to their homes! The king decreed that Ezra would lead the people back to Jerusalem. There they would rebuild the temple and worship the God of Israel.

Sometimes the people did not obey, but Ezra continued to lead by example.

I WILL LOVE AND OBEY GOD'S WORD.

Your Word Is a Lamp

Your Word is a lamp to my feet
And a light for my path wherever I am going.

MY SCRIPTURE SONG · MY SCRIPTURE SONG

CD 1
SONG 34

Heroes are leaders who love and obey God's Word. They lead by example and seek to please Him.

Gideon

"For my thoughts are not your thoughts, neither are your ways my ways," declares the LORD. ISAIAH 55:8

from JUDGES 6–8

GIDEON DID THINGS GOD'S WAY.

The Lord appeared to Gideon. He told Gideon that he would defeat the enemy army. Gideon's first battle was small, but he won! He and 10 men destroyed the enemy's altar. Then, to get ready for the big battle, Gideon gathered 32,000 men.

But God wanted them to win the battle His way. The enemy had about 135,000 men. God showed Gideon only 300 men He had chosen to fight. Gideon trusted the Lord. With a small band of 300 men, he defeated the huge army!

I WILL DO THINGS GOD'S WAY.

My Thoughts Are Not Your Thoughts

"For My thoughts are not your thoughts,
Neither are your ways My ways,"
Declares the Lord to all who will believe.

Heroes know that God's ways are not their ways. He wants us to depend on Him for the victories in our lives.

75

Habakkuk

I will be joyful in God my Savior.

HABAKKUK 3:18

HABAKKUK FOUND HIS JOY IN THE LORD.

from HABAKKUK 3

The prophet Habakkuk was joyful! He knew the secret of lasting happiness. It is not found in things you make or buy. Habakkuk knew that real joy and happiness come from loving and trusting the Lord.

Habakkuk taught that we should rejoice even if the fig tree does not bud. We should be happy even if there are no grapes on the vine, no sheep in the pen, or cattle in the stalls. We should rejoice because God is our God.

I WILL FIND MY JOY IN THE LORD!

Be Joyful

Hallelujah, hallelujah, Father!
Hallelujah, hallelujah, Lord!

Heroes are joyful because their happiness isn't found in how many things they have. It is found in knowing an amazing God!

Hannah

HANNAH BELIEVED IN A LISTENING GOD.

Hannah was heartbroken. She wanted a child but had not been able to have children. Yet Hannah believed that God could do anything! She went to the temple to pray. She asked God to bless her with a son. In return, she promised to give the child back to Him in service.

Hannah served a listening God! The Lord heard her prayer, and soon Hannah was blessed with a beautiful baby boy. She named him Samuel. Hannah joyfully dedicated Samuel to the Lord. He grew to become a great servant of the Lord.

I WILL BELIEVE IN A LISTENING GOD.

No One Holy Like the Lord

There is no one holy, holy like the Lord.
There is no one holy, holy like the Lord.

Heroes believe in a listening God! When they are troubled, they take it to the Lord in prayer. They know God always listens and answers!

Hezekiah

If my people . . . pray . . . then will I hear from heaven . . . and will heal their land. 2 Chronicles 7:14

from
2 KINGS 18–20

HEZEKIAH EXPECTED GOD TO ANSWER PRAYER.

As king of Judah, Hezekiah removed false gods and encouraged the people to pray and to worship God. He taught them to trust God for everything. As a result, God blessed the people.

Once Hezekiah became very ill. The prophet Isaiah told him the Lord said he would die. Hezekiah pleaded with God, "Remember, O Lord, how I have done what is good in Your sight." God answered Hezekiah's prayer by giving him 15 more years of life.

I WILL EXPECT GOD TO ANSWER PRAYER.

If My People Pray

MY SCRIPTURE SONG · MY SCRIPTURE SONG · CD 1 SONG 38

If My people who are called by My name will humble
Themselves and pray and seek My face and turn from
Their wicked ways, then I will hear from heaven.

*Heroes believe God can do anything, and they expect Him to answer
their prayers.*

81

Huldah

Speak the truth to each other.

ZECHARIAH 8:16

from
2 KINGS 22

HULDAH SPOKE GOD'S TRUTHS.

King Josiah lived in a time when the people in Jerusalem worshiped idols instead of God. When God's law was found, King Josiah learned that the people were committing great sins by worshiping idols. He felt terrible. He then sent Hilkiah the priest to a woman named Huldah, who was a prophetess.

God used Huldah to speak the truth. She said that God was about to bring disaster on Jerusalem because they had forgotten Him. But God promised not to bring the disaster as long as King Josiah ruled, because he humbled himself before the Lord.

I WILL SPEAK GOD'S TRUTHS.

Speak the Truth

MY SCRIPTURE SONG · MY SCRIPTURE SONG
CD 1
SONG 39

Speak the truth to each other. Speak the truth
To everyone. Speak the truth to each other,
And walk with your God beneath the sun.

*Heroes speak the truth of God when the news is good or even
when it is bad.*

Hur

Uphold me, and I will be delivered.

PSALM 119:117

from EXODUS 17:8–16

HUR HELPED GOD'S MAN
WHEN HE GREW TIRED.

The fighting was fierce. Joshua commanded the army of Israel as they fought Amalek. Moses, Aaron, and Hur watched the battle from the top of a hill. As long as Moses held up his hands, the Israelites would win. But when he lowered them, the Amalekites would win.

When Moses grew tired, Aaron and Hur got a stone for Moses to sit on. With Hur on one side and Aaron on the other, they held Moses' hands up in the air all day. With their help the battle was won.

I WILL HELP GOD'S PEOPLE
WHEN THEY GROW TIRED.

Uphold Me

Uphold me, and I will be delivered.
Uphold me, and I will be strong.

Heroes help others when they grow tired. Whether saying a kind word or cleaning a room, heroes are good helpers.

85

Isaac

from GENESIS 22

ISAAC TRUSTED AND OBEYED HIS PARENTS.

When Isaac was young, God asked Abraham, Isaac's father, to sacrifice his son. Isaac followed his father to a mountain, carrying the wood for the altar. Isaac asked Abraham, "Where is the lamb for the offering?" Isaac trusted and obeyed, even though he did not understand.

Abraham told his son that God would provide what they needed. Suddenly an angel said, "Don't hurt your son. You have shown your respect to God." Abraham then found a ram caught in the bushes and sacrificed it to God.

I WILL TRUST AND OBEY MY PARENTS.

Little Children, Obey

Children, won't you listen to me? I've got a song for you.
It's a verse right from the Bible
Teaching us what to do.

Heroes obey their parents in the Lord. This means they do the right things their parents ask, even when they may not understand.

Isaiah

For to us a child is born. . . . And he will be called Wonderful Counselor, Mighty God, Everlasting Father, Prince of Peace. ISAIAH 9:6

from the
book of ISAIAH

ISAIAH POINTED PEOPLE TO JESUS.

As God's prophet, Isaiah told the world about Jesus, the coming Messiah. There are as many as 121 prophecies about Jesus in the book of Isaiah. They tell us that He would be born of a virgin; He would heal the blind, deaf, and lame; He would die for the sins of the world; He would be buried in a rich man's tomb; and He would be resurrected by God. Isaiah told all of these things before Jesus was even born!

Isaiah spent his life pointing people to Jesus. We should too!

I WILL POINT PEOPLE TO JESUS.

Wonderful Counselor

Tell me, who do you call Wonderful Counselor?
O, O, O, O, glory hallelujah! O, O, O, O, glory hallelujah!
Glory hallelujah to the newborn King.

*Heroes point people to Jesus. They are not ashamed to tell others
about their Savior.*

Jabez

The Lord bless you and keep you; the Lord make his face shine upon you. NUMBERS 6:24–25

from 1 CHRONICLES 4

JABEZ ASKED GOD'S BLESSING ON HIS LIFE.

Jabez was an honorable man. He wanted to become a great man of God, and he knew exactly how to do it. He asked God's blessing on his life.

Jabez prayed for God to do good things for him. He asked God to give him more land, and to protect him. The Bible says God gave Jabez the desire of his heart.

I WILL ASK GOD'S BLESSING ON MY LIFE.

The Lord Bless You

The Lord bless you and keep you now.
The Lord make His face shine upon you
And be gracious, and be gracious, and be gracious to you.

*Heroes believe in a powerful and generous God. They know where
to go with the needs of their lives—straight to God in prayer.*

Jacob

I am with you . . .
wherever you go. GENESIS 28:15

from
GENESIS 28

JACOB TRUSTED GOD
TO WATCH OVER HIM.

Jacob was traveling to Haran. As he stopped to rest for the night, he fell asleep. He dreamed he saw a giant stairway, and the top reached all the way to heaven. Angels were climbing up and down the stairway.

High above it, God was watching. Then Jacob heard God speak, "No matter where you go, I will watch over you. I will be with you." Jacob woke up! "Surely the presence of the Lord is in this place," he said, "and I didn't know it!" From that point on, Jacob trusted God to protect his journeys.

I WILL TRUST GOD TO WATCH OVER ME.

God Will Be with You

The Lord your God will be with you wherever you go.
The Lord your God will be with you
Forever, child, yeah!

Heroes know that God is with them. He is watching over them.
God's watchful eye gives heroes courage to go through difficult times.

James,
the Brother of Jesus

*Is any one of you in trouble?
He should pray.* JAMES 5:13

from JOHN 7:5;
1 CORINTHIANS
15:7; ACTS 15

JAMES LIVED
WHAT HE BELIEVED.

He was the half-brother of Jesus, who could have been nicknamed "Camel Knees." The name "Camel Knees" means that James kneeled to pray so much, his knees were rough!

James didn't always believe Jesus was the Messiah. His friend John says that Jesus' own brothers did not believe in Him. But when Jesus appeared to James after He rose from the dead, James believed! He became a great church leader who wrote the book of James to teach us how to live like Jesus.

I WILL LIVE WHAT I BELIEVE.

We Should Pray

Is any one of you in trouble? Oh, he should pray,
He should pray. Is any one of you in trouble?
Oh, she should pray, she should pray.

Heroes live what they believe. They do the things that please Jesus.

95

James,
the Disciple

If anyone wants to be first, he must be the very last, and the servant of all. MARK 9:35

from
MARK 1; 5; 9; 14;
ACTS 12

JAMES WAS A
LOYAL SERVANT OF JESUS.

James and his brother, John, were fishermen, sons of a man named Zebedee. James gave up his fishing business to follow Jesus. He was one of Jesus' most loyal friends.

James was with Jesus when Moses and Elijah appeared on the mountain, when Jesus raised Jairus' daughter, and when Jesus prayed in Gethsemane. James even died for his faith in Jesus.

I WILL BE A LOYAL SERVANT
OF JESUS.

First

"I've got to be first," I used to say, but now
I'm learning a better way. I've got to be first,
And so to be, I'll let you stand in front of me.

Heroes are loyal servants. They follow Jesus no matter what it costs them.

Jason

Let us not love with words or tongue but with actions and in truth. 1 JOHN 3:18

from
ACTS 17:1–9

JASON PUT HIS LOVE INTO ACTION.

Jason lived in Thessalonica. When his friends Paul and Silas visited Thessalonica to preach the gospel, many came to believe in Jesus. This made some of the Jews angry. A mob gathered to look for Paul and Silas at Jason's house. Paul and Silas were not there, so the angry men had Jason arrested.

Jason put his love for the Lord and his friends into action. It seems that he allowed Paul and Silas to stay with him, even when it put him in danger.

I WILL PUT MY LOVE INTO ACTION.

Love in Action

Dear children, let us not love
With words or tongue,
But with action and truth.

Heroes put their love for others into action. They have the courage to do what is right.

Jehoshaphat

When I am afraid, I will trust in you.

PSALM 56:3

from
2 CHRONICLES 20

JEHOSHAPHAT BELIEVED THAT GOD WAS IN CONTROL.

A great number of enemy soldiers had come against Israel. But Israel had a wise leader named Jehoshaphat. He called the people together to pray and fix their eyes on the Lord!

God answered their prayers by speaking through Jahaziel, a Levite. He stood before Jehoshaphat and the people and said, "God is in control. The battle is not yours but the Lord's!" The very next day, the enemies were defeated!

I WILL BELIEVE THAT GOD IS IN CONTROL.

When I Am Afraid

When I am afraid, I will trust in You.
I will trust in You, my Father.

*Heroes keep their eyes fixed on the Lord, not on the circumstances.
No matter what kind of battle you are facing, God is in control!*

Jeremiah

"I know the plans I have for you," *declares the* LORD. JEREMIAH 29:11

from the book of JEREMIAH

JEREMIAH TRUSTED GOD'S PLANS FOR ISRAEL.

God had a job for Jeremiah. He needed Jeremiah to deliver a very difficult message to his people. Because of Jeremiah's great love for Israel, the message was very painful! He had to tell the people he loved that sorrow awaited them if they did not obey God. Jeremiah has become known as the "weeping prophet."

Even though the Israelites disobeyed God, Jeremiah still loved them. He knew they would be punished for their sin, and that made him sad. Jeremiah knew he must follow God's plan for him and deliver God's message. He trusted that his job was part of God's greater plan. And that plan included a better life to come for God's people.

I WILL TRUST GOD'S PLAN FOR ME.

The Plans I Have for You

For I know the plans I have for you, My little children.
For I know your plans, declares the Lord.

Heroes rely on God's wisdom and trust His plans. They know that if they just obey, God will work out the details.

103

Jesus

I am the good shepherd. The good shepherd lays down his life for the sheep. JOHN 10:11

from
JOHN 10

JESUS IS THE GOOD SHEPHERD.

Jesus is the greatest Bible hero of all! He called Himself the good shepherd. No name could be better.

People are like sheep in many ways. We get lost, and we lose our way. But like a good shepherd, Jesus comes looking for us. He leads us and protects us from our enemies. Most of all, He loves us. Jesus died on a cross so that we could live with Him forever. Little sheep, follow the good shepherd!

I WILL FOLLOW THE GOOD SHEPHERD.

I Am the Good Shepherd

I am the good shepherd. I am the good shepherd.
And the good shepherd lays down
His life for the sheep.

Heroes follow the greatest hero of all: Jesus, the good shepherd.

Jesus
as a Young Boy

I rejoiced with those who said to me, "Let us go to the house of the LORD." PSALM 122:1

from
LUKE 2:41–52

AS A YOUNG BOY, JESUS WENT TO GOD'S HOUSE.

When Jesus was 12 years old, Mary and Joseph took Him to Jerusalem to celebrate the Passover Festival. When it ended, Mary and Joseph started for home. After they had been traveling an entire day, they discovered Jesus was not in the crowd with them!

They returned to Jerusalem and found Him in the temple. The religious teachers were amazed at His answers to their questions. Jesus said to His mother, Mary, "Didn't you know that I had to be in My Father's house?"

I WILL GO TO GOD'S HOUSE.

We're Going to God's House Today

Wake up, sleepyhead, open your eyes. Birds are soaring
Through sunny skies. It's Sunday morning;
Let's not be late. We're going to God's house today!

Heroes know the importance of going to church. They love to hear God's Word and talk about it with other believers.

Jethro

Apply your heart to instruction and your ears to words of knowledge. PROVERBS 23:12

from EXODUS 18

JETHRO GAVE WISE, GODLY ADVICE.

Jethro was a priest and the father-in-law of Moses. He visited Moses and heard the great stories of how God performed amazing miracles and rescued the Israelites from the Egyptians. He rejoiced over all the good things the Lord had done.

Jethro also saw that Moses was very busy. Moses served as judge and teacher all day long. So Jethro said, "I will give you some advice." He instructed Moses to choose other trustworthy men and make them judges too. Moses listened to Jethro's good advice.

I WILL GIVE WISE, GODLY ADVICE.

Apply

Apply your heart to instruction and your ears to the
Words of knowledge. Listen to your teacher and
To the preacher. Wisdom I know you'll gain.

Heroes help by giving wise advice. When they see a problem, they
try to help solve it.

Job

Search me, O God, and know my heart; test me and know my anxious thoughts. PSALM 139:23

from the book of JOB

JOB LOVED GOD NO MATTER WHAT HAPPENED.

God had blessed Job with wealth and a large family. One day Satan appeared before God and said, "Job only loves You because he has such a good life. If things go badly for him, he will curse You instead."

Satan did everything he could to make Job hate God. He was allowed to make Job sick. He took away his children, his house, and everything that he owned. But Job said, "The Lord gives and takes away. Blessed be the name of the Lord." Job passed the test!

I WILL LOVE GOD NO MATTER WHAT HAPPENS.

Search Me

Search me, O God, and know my heart;
Test me and know my anxious thoughts.

Heroes may be tested by the Lord. Just remember, He tests the ones He loves.

Jochebed

The LORD will keep you from all harm—he will watch over your life. PSALM 121:7

from EXODUS 2

JOCHEBED TRUSTED GOD
TO KEEP BABY MOSES SAFE.

Many know Jochebed as the mother of Moses. She knew her baby son was very special, not only to her, but to God. Yet she had heard the mean king's order to kill all the Hebrew baby boys.

Acting in faith, Jochebed got a basket and sealed it. She put Moses in the basket and set it in the reeds along the bank of the Nile River. With a gentle push, Moses drifted into the loving arms of an Egyptian princess, where he would finally be safe.

I WILL TRUST GOD TO KEEP ME SAFE.

You Will Keep Us Safe

O, Lord, my Lord,
You will keep us safe.
You will protect us.

 Heroes trust God to watch over the ones they love. When they cannot be there, they know God is always there!

John

the Baptist

It is by the name of Jesus Christ . . . for there is no other name under heaven given to men by which we must be saved. ACTS 4:10, 12

from MATTHEW 3

JOHN THE BAPTIST DARED TO BE DIFFERENT AND FOLLOWED JESUS.

John the Baptist did not preach in a nice building. The desert was his church. It was hot and dusty without much to eat. But John the Baptist cared more about telling others about Jesus than anything! You could hear him shouting in the desert, "The Messiah is coming! Repent!" This he preached day after day.

John dressed a little differently. His clothes were made of camel hair. And he ate locusts and wild honey for dinner. But still people came to hear the preacher who was pointing the world to Jesus!

I WILL DARE TO BE DIFFERENT AND FOLLOW JESUS!

No Other Name

There is no other name under heaven
Given to men by which we must be saved.
O, there is no other name.

Heroes dare to be different and follow Jesus. They don't follow others; they follow truth!

115

John,
the Beloved Disciple

And this is love: that we walk in obedience to his commands. 2 JOHN 1:6

from the book of 2 JOHN

JOHN "WALKED THE TALK."

The greatest commandment is to love the Lord. The second greatest is to love your neighbor as yourself. The apostle John knew that love was more than talk. It was "walking the talk," or showing your beliefs through your actions.

Many times Jesus expressed His love in words. But He also died on a cross to show His love. John wrote a book of the Bible that answers the question, "How do we love?" We "walk the talk." We love as Jesus did!

I WILL "WALK THE TALK."

Walk in Obedience

"And this is love," said the Master.
"And this is love," said the Lord to all.
O that we walk in obedience to His commands!

Heroes "walk the talk." They obey the commandments of God as they walk in love.

Jonah

In my distress I called to the LORD, and he answered me. JONAH 2:2

from the book of JONAH

JONAH ADMITTED HE WAS WRONG WHEN HE DISOBEYED.

Jonah had disobeyed God. He was sailing to Tarshish instead of Nineveh, where God had commanded him to go. While at sea, a great storm arose. Knowing his disobedience had caused the storm, Jonah confessed to the others and was thrown overboard.

God rescued Jonah by allowing him to be swallowed by a great fish. But in the belly of the fish, he prayed to the Lord. God granted him a second chance. And this time, Jonah obeyed.

I WILL ADMIT THAT I'M WRONG WHEN I DISOBEY.

You Answered Me

In my distress I called to the Lord,
Called to the Lord, called, O called.

Heroes admit it when they make a mistake. They pray and seek forgiveness from God, and try never to make the mistake again.

Jonathan

A friend loves at all times.

PROVERBS 17:17

from
1 SAMUEL 18–20

JONATHAN WAS
A GOOD FRIEND.

After David fought the giant Goliath, he met Saul's son Jonathan. An amazing friendship began. They promised to be friends forever and defend each other against any enemy.

Because of David's growing popularity, Saul became very jealous. So he decided to kill David. But Jonathan remembered the promise he had made. He warned his friend, and David was able to get away safely.

I WILL BE A GOOD FRIEND.

A Friend Loves at All Times

O, a friend loves at all times. O, a friend loves at all times.
Morning, noon, or night, a friend is a delight,
For a friend loves at all times.

Heroes are good friends. They take care of each other. They defend each other. They love one another.

Joseph, the Son of Jacob

from GENESIS 37–50

JOSEPH FORGAVE HIS FAMILY.

Joseph's brothers were very jealous of him. The jealous brothers sold Joseph as a slave, but they told their father that a wild animal had killed him. Joseph's father was very upset.

As the years passed, God helped Joseph by giving him a special gift. He could tell others what their dreams meant. One day Joseph told Pharaoh that his dreams meant there would be a shortage of food. To prepare, Pharaoh made Joseph ruler over Egypt and put him in charge of storing food. When Joseph's brothers came to buy food, Joseph took care of them. He forgave his brothers.

I WILL FORGIVE MY FAMILY.

Brother, Where Art Thou?

O, brother, where art thou? Where have you gone?
I'm far away in Egypt 'cause you treated me wrong.

 Sometimes even the people in our family treat us unkindly. Heroes have a forgiving heart.

123

Joseph, the Husband of Mary

She will give birth to a son, and you are to give him the name Jesus, because he will save his people from their sins. MATTHEW 1:21

from MATTHEW 1

JOSEPH OBEYED GOD WITHOUT DELAY.

God had chosen Joseph and his wife-to-be, Mary, for important work. Jesus was coming, and they would be His parents. Mary would be the mother of God's own Son!

An angel told Joseph about God's plan in a dream. The angel said, "Mary's baby is from the Holy Spirit. Don't be afraid to marry her. Name the baby Jesus, because He will save His people from their sins." When Joseph awoke, he did just as the angel instructed.

I WILL OBEY GOD WITHOUT DELAY.

What Child Is This?

O Mary, O Mary, she will give birth to a son, a son,
And you are to give Him
The name, the name Jesus.

Heroes obey God without delay. Even when they don't fully understand God's plan, they trust and obey, knowing His plan is best for everyone.

Joseph
of Arimathea

I will turn their mourning into gladness; I will give them comfort and joy. JEREMIAH 31:13

from MATTHEW 27:57–60

JOSEPH SERVED THE LORD WITH WHAT HE HAD.

Joseph was a rich man from Arimathea. He was a follower of Jesus. After Jesus died, Joseph was surely very sad. Joseph asked Pilate for Jesus' body. Jesus had no burial place, so Joseph would give Him his own.

Joseph wrapped the body in linen cloth. He placed it in his tomb cut out of the rock. He rolled a big stone in front of it. Joseph didn't know that Jesus would only need it for three days! Soon his sadness would be turned to gladness.

I WILL SERVE THE LORD WITH WHAT I HAVE.

God Will Comfort Me

As a mother comforts her child, so will God comfort you.
As a mother comforts her child, so will God comfort you.

Heroes use what they have in service to the Lord. They know God will find a way to turn our gifts into great things.

127

Joshua

from
JOSHUA 5–6

JOSHUA CHOSE TO DO THINGS GOD'S WAY.

Joshua had seen Moses do things God's way. He had seen the Red Sea part and had eaten food that fell from heaven. Now the Israelites stood at the border of the Promised Land. Joshua would lead them in.

But the huge wall surrounding the city of Jericho must come down! God gave Joshua a battle plan: They would circle the city for seven days. Then the priests would give one long trumpet blast, and the people would shout! It seemed like a strange way to win a battle. Still, Joshua chose to do things God's way, and the victory was won!

I WILL CHOOSE TO DO THINGS GOD'S WAY.

Choose

Choose for yourselves this day whom you will serve.
But as for me and my household, we will serve the Lord.
We will serve the Lord. O, we will serve the Lord.

MY SCRIPTURE SONG • MY SCRIPTURE SONG • CD 2 SONG 12

Heroes make wise choices. They choose to do things the way God wants, no matter how strange it may seem.

Josiah

Remember your Creator in the days of your youth. ECCLESIASTES 12:1

from
2 KINGS 21–22;
2 CHRONICLES 34

THOUGH HE WAS YOUNG, JOSIAH SERVED THE LORD.

Josiah became king when he was only eight years old. His grandfather Manasseh was evil. Manasseh built altars for false gods and led the people away from God. But later Josiah became king and turned to the Lord.

The Bible says, "He did what was right in the eyes of the Lord." He had the idols destroyed. As workers were rebuilding the temple, Hilkiah the priest found the lost Book of the Law. It warned Israel that if they disobeyed God's Law, God would judge them. Josiah asked God to help his people.

STARTING NOW, I WILL SERVE THE LORD.

Remember Your Creator

Remember your Creator in the days of your youth.
Remember your Creator in the days of your youth.
And you will live a happy life. Amen.

Heroes are never too young to serve the Lord. They let no one look down on them because of their age.

Lois and Eunice

Train a child in the way he should go, and when he is old he will not turn from it. PROVERBS 22:6

from 2 TIMOTHY 1:1–8

LOIS AND EUNICE SHARED THEIR FAITH WITH THEIR FAMILY.

Timothy's grandmother Lois had a true faith. She shared that faith with her family. Later Timothy's mother, Eunice, shared it with her family. Then, when Timothy grew to be a young man, he carried that same true faith with him.

True faith is a real faith. It doesn't act one way in front of people and differently at home. The true faith of Lois and Eunice changed the life of Timothy. He became a friend of Paul the apostle and preached to many people!

I WILL SHARE MY FAITH WITH MY FAMILY.

Train Up a Child

Train up, train up, train up a child in the way he should go.
Train up, train up, train up a child in the way he should go.

Heroes have a true faith and share it with others. Their words and actions demonstrate to all that they genuinely trust God.

133

Lydia

How beautiful are the feet of those who bring good news! ROMANS 10:15

from ACTS 16:11–15

LYDIA HAD "BEAUTIFUL FEET."

Once Paul journeyed to Philippi to preach the gospel. On Saturday he and his friends went for a walk outside the city gate. They found some women gathered to pray. So Paul sat down and told them about Jesus.

A woman named Lydia was there. She was a businesswoman who bought and sold purple cloth. She accepted Jesus that day and was baptized. Lydia began serving Christ right then by inviting Paul and the other missionaries to stay at her home. She served them with gracious hospitality.

I WILL SEEK TO HAVE "BEAUTIFUL FEET."

How Beautiful

How beautiful are the feet of those who bring good news!
How beautiful are the feet of those who bring good news!

Heroes have "beautiful feet." That means that they go where they are needed and serve the Lord.

135

Mark

As iron sharpens iron, so one man sharpens another. PROVERBS 27:17

from ACTS 12:25–13:5; 1 PETER 5:13

MARK CHOSE GODLY FRIENDS.

Mark had a wonderful friend named Peter, who was one of the 12 apostles of Jesus. Peter was put in prison for preaching the gospel. It is thought that Mark visited him there and would write down what Peter told him about the life of Jesus. These writings became the Gospel of Mark.

Mark's cousin was Barnabas, who made a missionary journey with Paul. The godly example of friends like Peter, Paul, and Barnabas helped shape Mark's faith.

I WILL CHOOSE GODLY FRIENDS.

Iron Sharpens Iron

O, as iron sharpens iron, O, so one man sharpens another.
O, as iron sharpens iron, O, so one man sharpens another.

Heroes have godly friends. When we surround ourselves with godly people, they help us to be good and faithful.

137

Mary

What is impossible with men is possible with God. Luke 18:27

from
LUKE 1-2

MARY GAVE UP HER PLANS TO FOLLOW GOD'S PLAN.

Mary was engaged to a good man named Joseph. As she was making her wedding plans, God had different plans for her. The angel Gabriel went to Mary and told her the startling news: she was going to give birth to the promised Messiah!

Mary was the first to hear His name: Jesus! Though she did not understand it all, she said, "May God's will be done." Her wedding plans would have to wait. Jesus was coming soon!

I WILL FOLLOW GOD'S PLAN.

What Is Impossible with Men

What is impossible with men is possible with God,
My friend! Through it all, come thick or thin,
I'll believe it's possible with Him.

MY SCRIPTURE SONG • MY SCRIPTURE SONG • CD 2 SONG 17

Heroes are willing to give up their plans to follow God's plan. They know their sacrifice will be worth it.

Mary and Martha

from LUKE 10:38–42

MARY PUT GOD FIRST.

Mary and Martha were sisters. Though they both loved Jesus, they were very different. Martha was a doer. She prepared meals and cared for her home. Mary was a learner. She chose to listen and learn about her God.

One day Jesus came to visit. Martha, the doer, stayed busy. Mary, the learner, sat and listened to Jesus. Martha was upset that she wasn't helping. Martha burst into the room and demanded that Mary help. Jesus taught Martha that it is good to work, but it's better to learn about God.

I WILL PUT GOD FIRST.

Seek First

Seek first, seek first, seek first His kingdom.
Oh ya gotta seek first, seek first, seek first His kingdom
And His righteousness.

Heroes always put God first. They may enjoy other things, but they know that a relationship with God comes first.

Mary Magdalene

He is not here; he has risen.

MATTHEW 28:6

from
MARK 15:40–16:9

MARY MAGDALENE
WAS COMMITTED TO JESUS.

Mary Magdalene was a woman whose life had been changed. Jesus had saved her! After Jesus saved her, Mary Magdalene followed Him for the rest of her life.

She followed Jesus during His ministry. She followed Him to Calvary to witness the crucifixion. She followed Jesus to His tomb. She was among the first to hear the angel say, "He has risen." But perhaps her greatest joy was seeing the risen Savior!

I WILL BE COMMITTED TO JESUS.

Risen Indeed

Risen, He has risen! He has risen!
Allelu, allelu!
He is not here; He has risen indeed!

Heroes are committed to Jesus. They give their lives to sharing the good news and following His example.

Matthew

from LUKE 5:27–32

MATTHEW WAS WILLING TO LEAVE EVERYTHING TO FOLLOW JESUS.

Matthew, also known as Levi, was one of the 12 apostles. Before he followed Jesus, he was a tax collector. Tax collectors were hated by many people. One day Jesus saw Matthew sitting at his tax booth and said, "Follow Me." Matthew left and followed Jesus.

When some religious leaders saw Jesus eating at a banquet at Matthew's house, they asked, "Why does He eat with sinners?" Jesus answered, "It is not the healthy who need a doctor, but the sick. I have not come to call the righteous, but sinners to repentance."

I WILL BE WILLING TO LEAVE EVERYTHING TO FOLLOW JESUS.

Whoever Serves Me

MY SCRIPTURE SONG • MY SCRIPTURE SONG •
CD 2
SONG 20

Whoever serves Me must follow Me.
Follow Me. Hey! Hey!
Whoever serves Me . . .

Heroes are willing to give up everything to follow Jesus. When He calls, they follow willingly and leave the rest to Him.

145

Micah

MICAH HELPED OTHERS TO REMEMBER GOD'S COMMANDS.

Micah was a common man, but he was also God's prophet to Israel. He reminded the people of what God had done for them in the past. He spoke of a coming Messiah who would be born in Bethlehem.

Micah had a message for everyday living! He said to "act justly." This means to do what is right. He said to "love mercy," which means to care about others. And, he said to "walk humbly with our God." This means to believe God knows best and to follow Him. When Micah saw others heading in the wrong direction, he steered them back to what God said was right.

I WILL HELP OTHERS TO REMEMBER GOD'S COMMANDS.

Walk Humbly with Your God

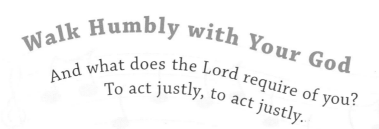

And what does the Lord require of you?
To act justly, to act justly.

Heroes know what the Lord requires of them: they must act justly.
They must do the right thing . . . and help others do the right thing too!

147

Miriam

Whoever can be trusted with very little can also be trusted with much. LUKE 16:10

from
EXODUS 2:3–10

MIRIAM COULD BE TRUSTED TO DO A JOB RIGHT.

Miriam was Moses' older sister. When Moses was a baby, Miriam took a big baby-sitting job. To save Moses from the wicked king, Moses' mother put him in a basket and set him in the tall grass along the bank of the Nile River. Miriam watched the basket.

A princess of Egypt found the basket and felt sorry for the baby. Miriam asked the princess, "Would you like for me to find a Hebrew woman to nurse him?" The princess answered yes, so Miriam went to her mother to tell her the good news. Moses' mother could still take care of him. Miriam had done her job well.

I WILL EARN TRUST BY DOING JOBS RIGHT.

Whoever Can Be Trusted

Whoever, whoever, whoever, whoever can be trusted
With very little—I know it's true!—
Can also be trusted with much. Can you?

Heroes can be trusted to do the job right. Whether big or small, they finish the task, giving it their best efforts.

Moses

Love the LORD your God with all your heart and with all your soul and with all your strength. DEUTERONOMY 6:5

from
EXODUS 19–20

MOSES LOVED THE LORD WITH ALL HIS HEART.

Moses' life was a great adventure. It was filled with miracles and mystery. But perhaps his greatest moment came when he met God on Mount Sinai. There Moses received the Ten Commandments.

God is love. So He gave Moses a list of ten things that loving people do and don't do. If you love your neighbors, you do not steal from them. If you love God, you do not serve false gods. Moses delivered God's love list to Israel. They would seek to obey!

I WILL LOVE THE LORD WITH ALL MY HEART.

With All Your Heart

God wants us to really love Him, love Him with all
Our hearts. Night or day, work or play, if you travel
Far away, it doesn't matter wherever you are.

Heroes love the Lord with all their hearts and their neighbors as themselves.

151

Naomi

from the book of RUTH

NAOMI LIVED A LIFE THAT REFLECTED GOD'S LOVE.

Naomi had two sons. While in Moab her sons married women named Ruth and Orpah. But Naomi's husband and sons died. Naomi was very sad. She decided to return to Judah. But because of the love Naomi had shown Ruth, Ruth did not want Naomi to go alone.

Following Naomi's loving example, Ruth went with Naomi to Judah and took care of her. Ruth soon married a man named Boaz, and they had a little baby who made Naomi's sad tears turn into joy.

I WILL LIVE A LIFE THAT REFLECTS GOD'S LOVE.

You Are the Salt of the Earth

You, you are the salt of the earth. You, you are the
Salt of the earth. If the salt loses its saltiness,
How can it be made salty again?

MY SCRIPTURE SONG · MY SCRIPTURE SONG

CD 2
SONG 24

*Heroes are a reflection of God's love. Their love and kindness give
others an example of God's love for us.*

Nathanael

from JOHN 1:45–49

NATHANAEL BELIEVED THAT JESUS WAS THE SON OF GOD.

Philip met Jesus and believed Him to be the Son of God. Philip went and found Nathanael sitting under a fig tree and said, "We have found the Messiah. He is Jesus of Nazareth." At first Nathanael did not believe, but he went with Philip to see Jesus.

Jesus saw Nathanael coming and said, "Look, here comes an Israelite who is always honest." Nathanael asked, "How do You know me?" Jesus answered, "Before Philip told you about Me, I saw you under the fig tree." Nathanael was now certain that Jesus was the Messiah!

I WILL BELIEVE THAT JESUS IS THE SON OF GOD.

Faith Is Being Sure

Faith is being sure of what we hope for,
And faith is being certain of what we do not see.
Faith is saying to the mountain, "Be moved! Be moved!"

Heroes believe with certainty that Jesus is the Son of God. They trust the Bible to be true and the Holy Spirit to confirm this in their hearts.

155

Nehemiah

Do not be anxious about anything, but in everything . . . present your requests to God. PHILIPPIANS 4:6

from the book of NEHEMIAH

NEHEMIAH PRAYED
BEFORE A BIG DECISION.

Nehemiah worked in a palace of the Persian king. When he learned that the wall of Jerusalem had been broken down and the gates burned, he wept. Nehemiah wanted to help rebuild the wall, but could not without the king's blessing.

Before he asked, he prayed, "O Lord, grant me favor with the king." Nehemiah then asked the king to allow him to go to Jerusalem. Seeing the sadness in Nehemiah's face, the king said, "Yes, Nehemiah, go and rebuild!"

I WILL PRAY BEFORE A BIG DECISION.

Do Not Be Anxious

Do not be anxious about anything,
But in everything . . . present your requests to God.

Heroes always pray before making big decisions. They ask God to guide them in the way they should go!

Nicodemus

from JOHN 3

NICODEMUS SOUGHT JESUS.

Nicodemus was a Jewish leader who wanted to help Jesus. He is called a "secret disciple" of Jesus because he came to see Jesus at night. Nicodemus said, "We know You have come from God." Jesus replied by saying, "You must be born again."

Nicodemus asked, "How can I do that?" When a baby is born, it changes places from inside the mother to outside. Jesus told him to change places. Change from living for yourself to living for God. Be born again! Nicodemus began to understand.

I WILL SEEK JESUS.

You Must Be Born Again

Hear this song; come sing along,
Loud and strong: you must be born again.

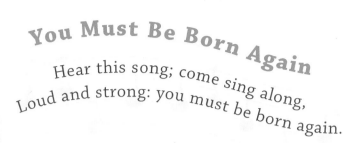
Heroes seek Jesus. They may seek Him in the morning. They may seek Him privately at night. But they always seek Him!

159

Noah

To obey is better than sacrifice.

1 Samuel 15:22

from
GENESIS 6–7

NOAH WAS OBEDIENT
WHEN GIVEN A DIFFICULT TASK.

Noah lived in a time when people ignored God. They chose to live selfish and sinful lives. But Noah loved God. God told Noah to build an ark, and Noah obeyed!

When the ark was completed, the animals entered it two by two. As the first raindrop fell, Noah's family and all the animals were already safe inside the ark. Soon the whole earth was flooded. But because of Noah's great love and humble obedience, God kept him and his family safe.

I WILL BE OBEDIENT
WHEN GIVEN A DIFFICULT TASK.

To Obey Is Better

To obey is better than sacrifice,
So obey the Lord, dear children.

Heroes love and obey the Lord. They know that genuine love goes hand in hand with obedience.

Paul

Go into all the world and preach the good news to all creation. Mark 16:15

from
ACTS 9:1–22

PAUL'S LIFE
WAS CHANGED BY JESUS.

Some Jewish leaders tried to stop Christianity. Saul of Tarsus, also named Paul, was such a leader. He had Christian men and women put in prison.

One day Saul was traveling on the Damascus Road. Suddenly he was surrounded by a blinding light. A voice said, "Saul, why are you so unkind to Me?" Saul asked, "Who are You?" He heard a reply: "I am Jesus." Saul was blind for three days. Then he became a Christian and started going by the name Paul. The man who once put Christians in prison became a great hero for Christ!

I WILL ALLOW MY LIFE
TO BE CHANGED BY JESUS.

GO!

Go into all the world
And preach the good news to everyone!

Heroes know that Jesus changes lives. He fills hearts with love and compassion for the lost.

Peter

Without faith it is impossible to please God. HEBREWS 11:6

from MATTHEW 14:22–32 **PETER STEPPED OUT IN FAITH.**

A mighty wind was blowing. The disciples were being tossed about in a boat. Suddenly they saw Jesus coming toward them, walking on the water. Peter shouted, "May I come to You?" "Come," Jesus said.

At that moment, Peter stepped out in faith. He stepped out of the boat and walked on the water. It was Peter's desire to go to Jesus, not just walk on water. Peter discovered that God will do miracles to get you closer to Jesus.

I WILL STEP OUT IN FAITH.

Without Faith

Without faith it is impossible to please God. (Repeat)
Well, I don't know why it's so, but the Bible says,
You know, without faith it is impossible to please God.

Heroes step out in faith. They keep their eyes on Jesus and trust the rest to Him.

Philip

from ACTS 6:5; 8:26–38

PHILIP WAS READY TO TELL OTHERS ABOUT JESUS.

Philip was one of seven men chosen by the disciples to serve the church in Jerusalem. One day an angel told Philip to go toward Gaza. As he went, he met an Ethiopian man reading the Scriptures. The man asked Philip, "Can you explain this?"

Because Philip knew the Scripture, he was ready to share the good news of Jesus with him. The Ethiopian then wanted to be baptized. When they came to some water, he had Philip baptize him. Philip was able to explain God's message and help the man understand what the Word says!

I WILL BE READY TO TELL OTHERS ABOUT JESUS.

Do Your Best, Child

Do your best, if you do it, child,
As if to the Lord.
No matter what the job, always do your best.

MY SCRIPTURE SONG • MY SCRIPTURE SONG

CD 2
SONG 31

Heroes are prepared to explain the gospel to those who are looking for the truth. God uses these heroes to spread the truth of His Word.

Phoebe

from
ROMANS 16:1–2

PHOEBE WAS A GOOD HELPER IN HER CHURCH AND COMMUNITY.

Phoebe had the gift of helping others. She loved the Lord and His church. Serving others was her great desire.

In his letter to the Romans, Paul recommends and praises Phoebe for helping him and many others. "I want to tell you good things about our sister Phoebe," he wrote. "Take care of her when she visits. She is a good woman." Phoebe must have been loved and respected by many people.

I WILL BE A GOOD HELPER IN MY CHURCH AND COMMUNITY.

A Good Name

A good name is more desirable
Than great riches, it's true!

Heroes are respected as good helpers in the community and in the church. When they see something that needs to be done, they do it.

Priscilla and Aquila

Love your neighbor as yourself.

MATTHEW 19:19

 **from ACTS 18:1–3; ROMANS 16:3–4**

PRISCILLA AND AQUILA SHOWED THE LOVE OF JESUS TO OTHERS.

Paul met Aquila and his wife, Priscilla, in Corinth. They were tent makers just like Paul. They also traveled with Paul on one of his mission trips. Paul faced many dangers and hardships on these journeys.

Though we do not know the details, Paul tells us of their great love. Priscilla and Aquila risked their very lives for him. Paul calls Priscilla and Aquila "fellow workers in Christ," who were ready to risk everything to tell others about Jesus. What a great love!

I WILL SHOW THE LOVE OF JESUS TO OTHERS.

Love Your Neighbor as Yourself

Love, love, la-la-la-la-la love
Your neighbor as yourself.

Whether telling others about Jesus in a far away place or being kind to the new kid at school, heroes show the love of Jesus to others.

Rahab

Our God is a God who saves.

PSALM 68:20

RAHAB SERVED A MIGHTY GOD WHO SAVES!

Before the battle of Jericho, Joshua sent two spies into the walled city. They came to the house of a woman named Rahab. She knew the men were spies from Israel. She had heard about the mighty things their God had done. She wanted to serve their God too.

She said to the two spies, "I know your God is mighty. When the battle comes, save my family and me." Rahab helped Joshua's men escape that night. When the battle came and the walls of Jericho fell, Rahab and her family were saved!

I WILL SERVE A MIGHTY GOD WHO SAVES!

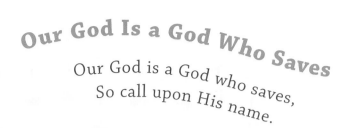

Our God Is a God Who Saves

Our God is a God who saves,
So call upon His name.

MY SCRIPTURE SONG • MY SCRIPTURE SONG
CD 2
SONG 34

Heroes serve a mighty God who saves. They realize how great God is and seek to serve Him.

Rebekah

Always try to be kind to each other and to everyone else. 1 THESSALONIANS 5:15

from GENESIS 24:1–27

REBEKAH WAS KIND.

Abraham wanted to find a wife for his son, Isaac. He told his main servant, "Go to my hometown. God will show you a bride for my son." When the servant arrived, he came to a spring. There he prayed that the young woman who comes and offers water to him and his camels would be the right girl for Isaac.

At that moment, Rebekah came near. She not only gave the servant a drink, but she kept returning to the well until all of his camels had plenty to drink. The servant had found the bride for Isaac!

I WILL BE KIND.

Be Kind

Be kind every day.
Be kind in every way.
Be kind to each other and everyone else.

Heroes are known for their kindness. It is the fruit of the Spirit that lets others know you care.

Rhoda

Be joyful always; pray continually; give thanks in all circumstances. 1 THESSALONIANS 5:16

from
ACTS 12:12–17

RHODA WAS JOYFUL AS SHE SERVED.

She worked long hours for John Mark's mother, Mary. Mary was a wealthy widow who opened her home to believers. One night believers had gathered there to pray for Peter. Suddenly there was a knock at the door.

When Rhoda heard Peter's voice, her joy overflowed. She ran to tell the others. She was so excited, she forgot to open the door and let Peter in! When they opened the door, there stood Peter. Everyone was amazed. Rhoda's joy was surely contagious.

I WILL BE JOYFUL AS I SERVE.

Be Joyful Always

Be joyful always; pray continually. Be joyful always;
Pray continually. Give thanks in all circumstances.
Give thanks to the Lord.

Heroes are joyful people. They serve the Lord with gladness.

Ruth

Where you go I will go, and where you stay I will stay. Your people will be my people and your God my God. RUTH 1:16

from the book of RUTH

RUTH LOVED NAOMI, EXPECTING NOTHING IN RETURN.

Ruth loved her mother-in-law, Naomi. Even after her husband died, Ruth decided to go with Naomi back to her home. Ruth expected nothing in return. She said, "Where you go, I will go. Your people will be my people and your God my God."

When they arrived in Judah, Ruth continued to care for Naomi. She gathered barley and wheat for them from the fields of a man named Boaz. God blessed Ruth's kindness. She and Boaz were soon married. They had a son named Obed, the grandfather of David.

I WILL SHOW LOVE TO OTHERS, EXPECTING NOTHING IN RETURN.

Where You Go, I Will Go

Where you go, I will go. Where you stay, I will stay.
And your people will be my people.
And your God will be my God.

Heroes love and appreciate others, expecting nothing in return.

Samson

I can do everything through him who gives me strength. PHILIPPIANS 4:13

from
JUDGES 13; 16

SAMSON ASKED GOD
TO GIVE HIM STRENGTH.

Manoah and his wife had no children. Then an angel brought them news that they would have a very special baby boy. Baby Samson was born and grew to be very strong. God's spirit was upon him.

But later in life Samson disobeyed the Lord, and his strength left him. In his final hour Samson prayed, "O Lord, remember me. O God, please strengthen me just once more." The Lord heard Samson's final prayer and restored his strength for one last victory over his enemies.

I WILL ASK GOD TO GIVE ME STRENGTH.

I Can Do Everything through Him

I can do everything through Him
Who gives me strength.

Heroes know their strength comes from the Lord. But if they disobey God, they can lose their power. To be strong in the Lord, we must obey!

Samuel

On my bed I remember you; I think of you through the watches of the night. PSALM 63:6

from
1 SAMUEL 3

SAMUEL ANSWERED
THE CALL OF GOD.

As a young boy Samuel served the Lord in the temple. One night Samuel was lying down when he heard a voice say, "Samuel." He ran to Eli the priest and said, "Here I am!" But Eli hadn't called for him. Samuel heard the voice a second and third time. But it wasn't Eli calling.

Eli realized that God was calling Samuel. He said to the boy, "If God calls again, answer, 'Speak, Lord. Your servant is listening.'" Samuel did as Eli said. God spoke to Samuel that night.

I WILL ANSWER THE CALL OF GOD.

On My Bed

On my bed I remember You;
I think of You through the watches of the night.

Heroes answer the call of God. They may not hear a voice with their ears, but their hearts know God is calling them to service.

Sarah

Is anything too hard for the LORD?

GENESIS 18:14

from GENESIS
18:1–15; 21:1–6

SARAH LEARNED THAT NOTHING
IS TOO HARD FOR THE LORD.

Sarah was Abraham's wife. All her life she had wanted a child. Then, when Abraham was 99 years old, the Lord said, "I make you this promise: you and Sarah will have a son."

Sarah heard what the Lord said, and she laughed. After all, they were too old to have children. When the Lord heard her laughter, He said, "Is anything too hard for the Lord?" At age 90 Sarah had a son. They named him Isaac, which in Hebrew means "he laughs."

I WILL BELIEVE THAT NOTHING
IS TOO HARD FOR THE LORD.

Is Anything Too Hard?

Is anything too hard for the Lord? There is nothing
He can't do. Have a little faith; believe it's true,
And you will find there's nothing He can't do.

*Heroes know that nothing is too hard for the Lord. He is able to do
the impossible for His glory.*

Shadrach, Meshach, and Abednego

Worship the Lord your God and serve him only. LUKE 4:8

from DANIEL 3

SHADRACH, MESHACH, AND ABEDNEGO DID THE RIGHT THING.

King Nebuchadnezzar set up a large golden statue. It was 90 feet tall and 9 feet wide. He commanded his people to kneel and worship the statue. But Shadrach, Meshach, and Abednego refused. They told the king they would only worship God.

The punishment for not bowing to the statue was death in a fiery furnace. Shadrach, Meshach, and Abednego put God first and did the right thing even as they were thrown into the fire! Suddenly a fourth man appeared in the fire with them. It was the Lord, who rescued and saved them.

I WILL DO THE RIGHT THING.

Worship the Lord

O, worship the Lord, your God.
O, worship the Lord, your God
And serve Him only.

Heroes put God first and serve Him, no matter what the cost.

Simeon

With the Lord . . . a thousand years are like a day. The Lord is not slow in keeping his promise. 2 PETER 3:8–9

from
LUKE 2:25–35

SIMEON TRUSTED GOD
TO KEEP HIS PROMISES.

God had promised Simeon that he would see the Messiah before he died. So Simeon watched and waited. One day God had Simeon go to the temple.

There he saw Mary and Joseph with baby Jesus. Like many Jewish parents, they brought Jesus to the temple to be dedicated to the Lord. Mary let Simeon hold baby Jesus. Simeon said, "Now I can die in peace, for I have seen the Savior."

I WILL TRUST GOD TO KEEP HIS PROMISES.

A Thousand Years Are Like a Day

Do not forget this one thing: with the Lord a day is
Like a thousand years. Do not forget this one thing:
And a thousand years are like a day.

MY SCRIPTURE SONG • MY SCRIPTURE SONG • CD 2 SONG 42

Heroes trust God to keep His promises. They know God will do what He says, and they trust their lives to His promises.

189

Simon of Cyrene

from MARK 15:21

SIMON OF CYRENE SHARED THE BURDEN OF ANOTHER.

There was a man from Cyrene who was visiting Jerusalem. Coming in from the fields, he heard the noise of a crowd. Jesus was passing by carrying a heavy cross.

Seeing that Jesus might collapse under the weight of the cross, the soldiers forced Simon to help Jesus. They laid the cross on him. Simon helped Jesus carry the cross.

I WILL SHARE THE BURDENS OF OTHERS.

Follow Me

If anyone would come after Me,
He must deny himself and take up his cross—
Deny himself, forgetting the cost.

Heroes help Jesus. They may not carry a heavy wooden cross, but they bear a different cross—the task of helping to win the lost!

Solomon

from 1 KINGS 3

SOLOMON ASKED GOD FOR WISDOM.

Solomon was the son of King David. Before David died, Solomon became king. God came to Solomon one night and said, "Ask for whatever you want Me to give you." Solomon asked God to give him wisdom to lead Israel.

God was pleased with Solomon because he did not ask for selfish things like wealth or power. So God promised Solomon not only wisdom but riches and honor as well. Soon Solomon was known as the wisest man in all the world.

I WILL ASK GOD FOR WISDOM.

The Fear of the Lord

The fear of the Lord is the beginning of wisdom,
So start with the Lord.

Heroes ask God for wisdom. They know how important it is in making good decisions. With wisdom, we can do the right thing!

Stephen

Forgive as the Lord forgave you.
COLOSSIANS 3:13

from
ACTS 6–7

STEPHEN FORGAVE THOSE WHO TREATED HIM UNFAIRLY.

Stephen was a leader in the early church. He was full of God's power. He did great miracles and told everyone that Jesus is God's Son. The people began to follow Jesus, which made some Jewish leaders angry.

Even though Stephen did nothing wrong, the religious leaders decided to kill him! Stephen had told them they had not obeyed God's Law. Even as people were throwing stones to kill him, Stephen asked God to forgive them.

I WILL FORGIVE THOSE WHO TREAT ME UNFAIRLY.

Forgive, Forgive

Forgive, forgive, forgive as the Lord forgives you.
Forgive, forgive, forgive as the Lord forgives you.

When heroes are treated unfairly, they forgive. They can forgive because they know they have been forgiven.

The Tenth Leper

Give thanks to the LORD, for he is good.
His love endures forever. PSALM 136:1

from LUKE 17:11–19

ONE OF THE MEN SAID, "THANK YOU."

A group of ten men had leprosy. Leprosy is a skin disease. In the Bible, those who had leprosy weren't allowed near healthy people until the priest said they were healthy again.

When the ten lepers saw Jesus, they called to Him, "Have pity on us!" Jesus saw their disease and said, "Go show yourselves to the priest." While they were going, they were healed. They were so happy! But only one of the men turned back to say "Thank You" to Jesus. Jesus was pleased with his thankfulness and faith.

I WILL SAY, "THANK YOU!"

Give Thanks to the Lord

O, give thanks to the Lord,
For He is good, He is good.

Heroes thank Jesus for what He has done. He can take away our sicknesses, and He can take away our sin!

197

Thomas

I am the way and the truth and the life. No one comes to the Father except through me. JOHN 14:6

from
JOHN 20:24–29

THOMAS PROCLAIMED
HIS FAITH IN THE LORD.

Thomas walked with Jesus. He watched as Jesus healed people who couldn't walk and made blind eyes see again. He saw Jesus calm a storm by just speaking. Thomas saw Jesus do many miraculous things!

But no one could die on a cross and come back to life again, he thought. No one! Then Jesus stood before Thomas. "Touch My hands and side," He said. "Believe!" Thomas was sorry that he had not believed! Now he knew that Jesus was "the Way."

I WILL PROCLAIM MY FAITH IN THE LORD.

I Am the Way

I am the Way, the Truth and the Life.
No one comes to the Father except through Me.

Heroes proclaim their faith. And heroes make mistakes. But when they do they are quick to confess their faults.

Timothy

Don't let anyone look down on you because you are young, but set an example for the believers. 1 TIMOTHY 4:12

from
ROMANS 16;
1 & 2 TIMOTHY

TIMOTHY SERVED THE LORD IN HIS YOUTH.

Timothy lived in a Roman village called Lystra. Paul visited there on his first missionary journey. Timothy's mother, Eunice, and his grandmother Lois most likely heard Paul's preaching and became Christians at that time. Paul felt that Timothy had his mother and grandmother's same great faith.

Timothy was young when he became a believer. Though he faced many temptations, his faith was strong. Paul met Timothy on his second visit to Lystra and asked him to come along. Timothy became a great evangelist!

I WILL SERVE THE LORD IN MY YOUTH.

Because You Are Young

MY SCRIPTURE SONG · MY SCRIPTURE SONG
CD 2
SONG 48

Set an example for believers in life.
Set an example for believers in love.
Set an example for believers in faith.

Heroes can serve the Lord at a very young age. They know that serving the Lord means that we always put Him first.

Zacchaeus

All have sinned and fall short of the glory of God. ROMANS 3:23

from LUKE 19:1–10

ZACCHAEUS LET NOTHING KEEP HIM FROM KNOWING JESUS.

Zacchaeus was a short man. He was a tax collector and had become rich from cheating people. When he heard that Jesus was coming to Jericho, Zacchaeus wanted to see Him.

Zacchaeus was so short, he couldn't see over the crowd. He ran ahead and climbed up a sycamore tree. Then he could see Jesus! As Jesus passed, He called out to Zacchaeus, "Come down. I must stay at your house!" Down he came. That day Zacchaeus was saved!

I WILL LET NOTHING KEEP ME FROM KNOWING JESUS.

The Romans Road

For all have sinned
And fall short of the glory of God.

 Heroes let nothing keep them from knowing Jesus. Seeking Jesus may be difficult, but He will help us when we follow Him.

Zenas

Grow in the grace and knowledge of our Lord and Savior Jesus Christ. 2 PETER 3:18

from TITUS 3:13

ZENAS USED HIS KNOWLEDGE
TO DEFEND THE FAITH.

Zenas is a little-known follower of Jesus. He is mentioned only once in the Bible. He is called "the lawyer" in a letter Paul wrote to Titus. Zenas was like an expert in rules.

Paul may have sent him to churches to help settle arguments and defend the faith. Though little is known about Zenas, we think he used his wisdom and knowledge to defend the faith.

I WILL USE MY KNOWLEDGE
TO DEFEND THE FAITH.

Grow in Grace and Knowledge

Grow in the grace and knowledge
Of our Lord and Savior Jesus Christ.

Heroes use their knowledge to defend the faith. They are armed with facts, and even bring others to believe.